Mary's Answer for
Our Troubled Times

Gerald Vann, O.P.

Mary's Answer for Our Troubled Times

SOPHIA INSTITUTE PRESS®
Manchester, New Hampshire

Mary's Answer for Our Troubled Times is a reprint of *At the Foot of the Cross: The Seven Lessons of Mary for the Sorrowing Heart* (Manchester, New Hampshire: Sophia Institute Press, 1998), with revised chapter titles and a new publisher's note. This 2002 edition by Sophia Institute Press is published with the permission of HarperCollins Publishers. The Author asserts the moral right to be identified as the Author of this work.

On the cover: Foreground image: *The Virgin in Prayer*, Sassoferrato
© National Gallery, London, UK/Bridgeman Art Library;
background photograph: *September 21, 2001* © Corbis Sygma.

Sophia Institute Press®
Box 5284, Manchester, NH 03108
1-800-888-9344
www.sophiainstitute.com

Imprimi Potest: Fr. Hilary J. Carpenter, O.P., *Prior Provincialis Angliae*
London, July 18, 1950
Nihil Obstat: Francis Diamond, *Censor Deputatus*
Imprimatur: Leo, *Episcopus Northantoniensis*

Library of Congress Cataloging-in-Publication Data

The Library of Congress has catalogued an earlier edition
of this work as follows:

Vann, Gerald, 1906-1963.
    At the foot of the cross : the seven lessons of Mary for the sorrowing
    heart / Gerald Vann.
        p. cm.
    Rev. ed. of: The seven swords. 1953.
    Includes bibliographical references.
    ISBN 0-918477-65-4 (pbk. : alk. paper) — ISBN 1-928832-54-7 (pbk. :
    alk. paper)
    1. Sorrows of the Blessed Virgin Mary, Devotion to. I. Vann, Gerald,
    1906-1963. Seven swords. II. Title.
    BX2161.5.S6V3   1998
    232.91 — dc21   97-46620 CIP

01 02 03 04 05 06 07 08 09 10 9 8 7 6 5 4 3 2 1

Contents

Publisher's note

Terror like this is not new.

Nor is the way in which men wield it as a weapon, even against the innocent.

Not sixty years ago, terror rained death from above onto the citizens of London, taking suddenly and without warning the wife who paused too long at the fruit stand, the grandfather feeding pigeons in the park, and the child laughing as he threw sticks for his dog.

When the bombs began falling mercilessly on London, ordinary citizens quickly learned a lesson that men and women in less-civilized societies had long known well: too easily we place our trust in the things of this life, but those things pass quickly away, and we with them. Now is the time to turn to God.

Among the souls whom terror instructed in this wisdom was the British priest Gerald Vann, who recognized in the evil of his time, rampant and wanton, the same evil that sought the life of the Child Jesus and that, all her days, sought to harm Mary and those she loved.

Fr. Vann saw in Mary's answer to the evils she endured a lesson, intended by God, for suffering souls in his time, in our time, and for all times.

These pages, written not long after the Nazi reign of terror, reveal to us how, two thousand years ago, God, in His ineffable Providence, gave us the life of the Virgin as a sure answer to the sudden terrors of our day.

*Mary's Answer for
Our Troubled Times*

The prophecy of Simeon

Mary shows us how to let love conquer fear

And Simeon said to Mary, "Thy own soul a sword shall pierce."

Luke 2:34, 35

We live in days that are shadowed by fear. There are the private, personal fears, as there always have been: of pain, of illness, of death, of the loss of those we love, and of the coming of misfortune and tragedy to those we love. But behind all these private fears, there looms like a sinister backdrop the despair and misery of the world at large: the sense of foreboding, the feeling that disaster is imminent and will not be averted. And because these fears can make us gloomy and uncreative, robbing us of our energy — can make us despair, forgetting God — it may well follow that we, for our part, bring disaster nearer. For despair invites it, being the will-to-death; only faith, hope, and love can combat it, being the will-to-life. That is why fear, of any kind, is not something to be simply escaped from and as far as possible forgotten, but something to be faced, understood, and transformed. And as in all our sorrows we can learn from Mary's sorrows, so in all our fears we can learn from Mary's fear.

Mary's Answer for Our Troubled Times

"Thy own soul a sword shall pierce." Simeon's words are not the first reference to fear in her life: at the very beginning of the story, she is told, "Fear not," as her destiny is announced to her.[1] For indeed, it is a destiny which must fill her heart with dread the more deeply she penetrates its meaning, and the more clearly she begins to see what redemption must mean for herself and her Son, to see the shadows of the Cross closing in on Him, and to understand what Evil will do to Him.

And yet, as we watch this life overcast by fears so immeasurably greater than ours, we are struck, not by any timidity or shrinking or sense of desperation, but by courage and strength and joy; and perhaps the courage and strength we can more readily understand, but how can we understand the joy? Yet she sings to Elizabeth of her joy at the things that are done in her;[2] she is the mother, glad as she cuddles her Child — divinely glad, for her divine Child; she joins in the joys of the wedding at Cana;[3] and although when she takes Him once again on her lap when all is over, it is only the heartbroken

---

[1] Luke 1:30.

[2] Luke 1:46-55: the *Magnificat*.

[3] John 2:1.

6

woman we are conscious of, still we are not to suppose that the *Magnificat* was but the expression of a swiftly passing mood: the sword is always there, but so is the song. What is the secret of it?

The Church, in Her devotion to Mary, lays great emphasis on the fact that, in her motherhood, she remained maiden as well. We shall miss all the richness of this mystery if we think of this insistence as being purely or even primarily concerned with the physical. Motherhood produces fundamental psychological changes in a woman: it means normally the end of one life and the beginning of another; it means the loss of some qualities and the acquisition of others, a different mentality, a different outlook. The mother has known the deep experiences of love and joy, of pain and danger and sorrow: we think of her as the symbol of wisdom because she has known in her own body the mysteries of good and evil.

The girl, on the other hand, is the symbol of opposite qualities: of a freshness and spontaneity and purity of heart which come precisely from inexperience, knowing only that reality can be ugly, not yet made wise through the lessons of sorrow: her courage, her strength, her wisdom, and her joy are from other sources.

Mary's Answer for Our Troubled Times

And in Mary alone, the Maiden-Mother, these opposite sets of qualities coexist; it is this that gives her personality a richness which is unique; and it is because of this richness that she can teach us so much.

First of all, we must see in her the twofold fear. We must see the fear of the mother, based on the experience of known evil, the human ugliness which life has already revealed, as a mother feels her child's physical dangers in her own nerves and bones because she has already known them or their like in her own experience. And we must see the fear of the girl, sensing an evil that is all the more difficult to meet because it is unknown: sensed as an enemy because it is wholly alien, wholly unnatural; sensed as a danger in the way the evil presences and emanations of the ghost stories inspire in those who feel them the terror of the unknown.

Mary's life, then, is a song at once of innocence and of experience; and as this double richness means a double fear, so it means also a double love; and the love, in its turn, produces a double wisdom, a double trust, and therefore a double courage. "Mary pondered all these things in her heart":[4] it is her song of her experience,

4 Luke 2:19.

and the source of her mother-wisdom. She knew how He that is mighty had done great things in her; she knew the overshadowing power of the Most High;[5] she knew the gradually unfolding self-revelation of her Son. And knowing these things, she could sense the Resurrection through the Cross, the joy through the pain, the triumph through the failure; and so she could find the courage to meet the sword.

"Behold the handmaid of the Lord":[6] there, on the other hand, is her song of innocence: whatever may come, it will be well, because it is His will, because He is Love: hers are eyes, too, that can look out untroubled on a future which is wholly veiled, simply because she has implicit trust in the God she loves, even before the trust has been justified by experience; and as the mother can say, "I can do all things in Him who has strengthened me," so the girl can say, "I can do all things in Him who *will* strengthen me."[7]

But this love produces more than wisdom and trust and courage. We are told that perfect love drives out

---

[5] Luke 1:49, 35.

[6] Luke 1:38.

[7] Cf. Phil 4:13.

fear;[8] but it does not leave a vacuum behind it: it leaves joy in its place. Once assured of the ultimate outcome, the mother's fears are turned into joy because she can share in her Son's ordeal; she can help; she is part of His vocation. The girl's fears are turned into the joy which is part of her pride in taking His life to herself. More than that, there is, in each case, the joy in a love which is itself a sustaining strength; and more than that again, the love that is strong enough to cast out fear is strong enough also to inspire that purely selfless joy in its object which is known to us selfish sinners far more in the relatively impersonal appreciation of the beauty of art than in the more personal and passionate appeal of human relationships. And as in Mary the Mother there is, unsullied by possessiveness, the mother's pride and joy in her Child, so in Mary the Maiden there is, unsullied by any self-regardingness, the girl's awe and joy in a Beauty and a Love whose infinite loveliness she can only adore.

What, then, must we do if we are to be freed from our fears? First of all, we can try to imitate Mary the Mother. We can try to learn something of her wisdom. In prayer,

[8] 1 John 4:18.

we can ponder God's power and God's pity: again and again, in the loosing of our sins, we have had experience of it; we need to deepen our awareness of that experience, so that the sense of the divine enfolding arms is always with us, and colors our judgments of immediate dangers and disasters, and helps us to see always, as Mary saw, the resurrection beyond the cross. So we shall come to have something of her trust in Him who is mighty; and with her trust, her courage; and with her courage, her joy — a joy not merely from this divine sense of security but also, and more deeply, from the fact that, forgetting our own fears, we can share in His redeeming work as she shared in it, and perhaps can even know some faint stirrings of that yet diviner joy which is her selfless pride in her Child.

But what of the wisdom of Mary the Maiden? How, in our sinfulness, can we hope ever to imitate that? How can we ever hope to recapture the qualities of a soul unravished by sin when sin, in fact, is so domiciled in our souls? We shall perhaps find an answer if we reflect that there is one kind of fear which is not something we need to be freed from, but something we need to acquire. Mary could not but fear the Cross; but far more, she feared the sin that caused the Cross. We, for our part, know all too well the misery of the world which is caused by the evil in the world, but of that evil itself we have so little sense, so little dread. And so our own sinfulness goes to increase the weight of evil and therefore, in some sense, the weight of misery. If we could we have Mary's fear of sin, we would reverse the process: the growing sense of sin would increase our sorrow, and therefore our love, and therefore our sense of the beauty and love and pity of God. And so we would share in the divine process of driving back the evil, of conquering the evil; and we would be helping to lessen not only the sin, but the misery of the world.

But the difficulty remains. In Mary the Mother, there is the dread of sin based upon bitter experience — not, of course, in her own soul, but in the souls of others — knowing the evil thing in itself, knowing its effects in misery, degradation, hatred, and destruction. But in Mary the Maiden, the dread is something quite different, as we have seen: the dread of something unknown, wholly alien, the dread of something sensed but not experienced as evil because it is unnatural, something from another, darker world. And so the question again presents itself: How are we to hope to imitate that? Can a soul recapture its lost innocence?

Mary shows us how to let love conquer fear

To study the lives of the saints who have once been sinners is to be compelled to answer yes. And this includes not only the saints who have never gravely sinned, but all the saints who have about them precisely that quality of freshness, of youth of soul, of a simplicity so unlike the duplicities and complexities in which sin involves us, which we thought of as characterizing the girl-symbol. With them, as with us, the experience is there; it lives on. But whereas it makes us old and seared and tawdry in heart, in them it is transmuted into something so different that sin becomes for them not an old and constant companion whose every feature is familiar, but a fraud unmasked, an enemy revealed in his true colors, the alien of the virgin-saints seen and sensed as such.

And how has this come about? Because sorrow for sin is creative: it has so increased their love of God, and it has brought them so close to God, that they become like to God. And the man who is like to God is strange to sin.

It is not enough, then, to say that a growing sense of sin means a growing love of God and therefore a growing joy in God: we must say also that it means a growing closeness to God and therefore the recapturing of a primal innocence, with the special wisdom, strength, trust, and joy which that innocence carries with it.

And so it becomes quite clear what we must do if we wish to imitate Mary in her twofold richness of life. First, we must ponder these things in our hearts: to try to understand more deeply what God does to share in and cure man's sorrows and sins, and what we, for our part, have done so differently; and so to find true creative sorrow and the love and the wisdom that spring from it.

But then, secondly, we must begin to say, "Behold the handmaid of the Lord": and this is something we can say no matter what history of accumulated evil may lie behind, provided only that now we begin to know and acknowledge our nothingness and helplessness, and destroy all the self-fashioned and self-imposed masks we have presented to ourselves and to the world, and stand naked under the creative and re-creative hand of God. Be it done unto me: done from the very beginning, for there is nothing here but the negation of light and life; nothing therefore that can give any direction, have any rights, form any pattern; no power, no entity, no I, but only the dark chaos of a nothingness out of which God, but only God, can create a real man. Be it done unto me,

14

then, in order that now, at long last, there may *be* an I, and all the old falsehoods and fictions of pride and vanity may be swept away. And so the new I is indeed something new, newborn, a beginning of life. And although the old experiences are there still, they begin to lose their power; they cease to be the driving force, to color all the thoughts of the mind and the desires of the heart: we are become what St. Peter calls us, "the first-born of creation,"[9] and in the fresh, vivid light of the new dawn, our eyes are opened and we see; we see now with something of the vision of unsullied youth; we see a new Heaven and a new earth.[10]

"The eyes of the saint make all beauty holy, and the hands of the saint consecrate everything they touch to the glory of God, and the saint is never offended by anything and is scandalized by no man's sin because he does not know sin. He knows nothing but the love and mercy of God, and he is here on earth to bring that love and that mercy to all men."[11]

[9] Cf. Col. 1:15.

[10] Cf. 2 Peter 3:13; Rev. 21:1.

[11] Thomas Merton, *Seeds of Contemplation* (Norfolk, Connecticut: New Directions Books, 1949), 21.

Mary's Answer for Our Troubled Times

How can he not be scandalized? How can he not know? Because now there is no common ground: there is no sin to call to sin, no abyss in him to answer the abysses of evil; sin has ceased to be connatural to him and is become alien like a foreign tongue.

The flight into Egypt

Mary shows us how to bear sudden losses

And behold an angel of the Lord appeared in sleep to Joseph, saying, "Arise, and take the Child and His mother, and fly into Egypt; and be there until I shall tell thee."

Matthew 2:13

In recent times, England has become a land of refuge for many exiles.[12] Germans, Austrians, Jews, Poles, political refugees from many another country: all have found refuge in England and a home. And surely we may hope that their harboring may bring upon us a blessing. In the Middle Ages, men sought safety from pursuit in the sanctuary, the holy place; and the fact that men of today can find sanctuary in England may help, we may hope, to make it a holy place itself in the end. But for these refugees, although it means safety, it must still be *terra aliena,* "a strange land": they have been uprooted; their own land, traditions, ways, and possessions are lost to them, are left behind; and they know not only the poverty of dispossession but the sorrow of homesickness.

This Gospel scene of the flight into Egypt is like so many contemporary stories that it must seem particularly vivid to us. The night, the darkness, the sudden

[12] Fr. Vann is speaking of the late 1940s. — ED.

preparations, and the departure into the unknown, the strange, and the perilous; the parents, anxious for their Child's safety, and the Maiden-Mother with her double fears; and Egypt itself the symbolic land of darkness, of exile, of the prison camp: the whole story is a symbol, not of an adventure, a conquering of new territory, but of a loss.

The natural right to property is based on a solid fact: that the human personality is not contained within the confines of the physical body. To be fully alive, a man must have a setting. The personality is expressed and fulfilled through its extensions: through creative work, human relationships, home, family roots and traditions, and through the native soil, native land, and native culture. The word *tradition* means a handing on; it is a double process: a receiving from those who have gone before and a passing on to those who are to come. And where a tradition is really living, it must in consequence change from generation to generation; it must be enriched by the thought and the labors of each succeeding age. And it is in that work of adapting and enriching a material environment that man's personality reaches its natural completion. That is why patriotism, the love of the *patria* — and we may take it here as including all that we mean by *home* — is a virtue: not nationalism, not enmity or pride or aggressiveness in regard to other nations, but a reverence and gratitude for the gifts that have come down to us, a love of our particular way of life and of the land in which the family tree is rooted and the family ways were begotten: "this little world, this precious stone set in the silver sea . . . this blessed plot, this earth, this realm, this England. . . ."[13]

Yet it remains true that possessions, even these possessions, are a danger. Material property can imprison and enslave us; patriotism can degenerate into insularity and narrow-mindedness; the setting can become not an enlargement of personality but an encircling wall. That is why Christianity upholds the right to property but, at the same time, preaches the virtue of poverty of spirit.[14] Life must have its dignity, and you must love the things that are worthy of love; but you must remain free. And sometimes the tyranny of material things can become so complete that it makes the love of God impossible: and either you must flee these things, or you flee God. So it is that St. Thomas says of the flight into Egypt: "He

[13] William Shakespeare, *Richard II*, act 2, scene 1.
[14] Matt. 5:3.

willed this flight that He might thereby bring back those who flee from the face of God." It is the symbol of that evangelical poverty, that giving up of material possessions, which is an assertion of the primacy of primary things.

Good living, comfort, pleasure, money, home, country: all these may, if we let them, become a flight from God, an attempt to forget Him and His demands. And the more valuable they are in themselves, the more dangerous they may be to our self-deceiving minds:

> *I fled Him down the nights and down the days;*
> *I fled Him down the arches of the years;*
> *I fled Him down the labyrinthine ways*
> *Of my own mind; and in the mist of tears*
> *I hid from Him, and under running laughter.*[15]

Sometimes it is a distraction unrealized for what it is until its empire is established, and sometimes it is a way of forgetting which, consciously or unconsciously, we deliberately seek. In either case, we find ourselves in the end enslaved.

We need, then, in some form or another, a flight into Egypt to save us from idolatry and degradation. "Arise,

[15] Francis Thompson, "The Hound of Heaven," Part 1.

and take the Child": and it was to be at once, and it was to be by night. That is poverty of spirit: to love the things that God has given you to complete your life, but to be ready to give them back to Him if He requires them, and to give them at once — not grudgingly, not with reservations and grumblings, but readily, eagerly, if possible joyfully — and to give them back even though it is in the darkness, even though there seems no sense in it and the future is black and the world seems, in consequence, empty and cold.

"Poor banished children of Eve" we call ourselves in the *Salve Regina*; and there are moods, when the sun is shining and the earth is lovely and life is good, in which it seems very unreal; but the words are expressing not a mood but a fact. Our job is to live our life here as well as we can by doing God's will for us as well as we can: and that will includes many things that are lovely, which we must love; many joys which we must take gratefully and gladly from His hands; many things which are not transitory and fleeting but eternal, and will remain a part of us always; the knowledge and wisdom and love that life may bring us. But nonetheless it remains true that the setting as a whole, the material setting, is transitory, is fleeting, is not ultimately home. The human home that endures is not this house, this garden, these material things, but these human beings whom you love and the mutual love in which you all live and which makes you all a single entity.

"Take the Child and His mother, and be there until I shall tell thee": it is not only the going but the staying that God's will determines and that is part of our obedience. And that means two things: it means not clinging to good things when God requires them of us; and it means also not being impatient to escape from bad things when God requires them of us. Egypt is the land of darkness. For some the sojourn in the darkness is a long one, perhaps seemingly an unending one; even the sunniest lives have their times of darkness. In either case, these things have their purpose if only we can see it and welcome it: they are teaching us to be poor in spirit; they are teaching us not to be tyrannized over; they are teaching us to be free; they are teaching us the primacy of primary things; and they are teaching us not to flee God, who is our home.

But traditionally, too, the land of darkness is a land of peril, filled with evil powers and presences who seek to destroy. Sometimes it seems relatively easy to love God and to do His will, but there are the black moods, the times when the dark waters seem to be closing over us, when we seem to turn inescapably to evil thoughts and things, when we have a devil, and when the evil powers are abroad in the darkness. It is then that, unless we have learned to be poor in spirit, the material world can turn on us and rend us, drag us down and humiliate us, and blot out altogether the presence of God. For the black moods are, in fact, an uprising from the human underworld within us, an uprising which reduces — perhaps for a time almost to nothing — the power and authority of the spirit; and it is then especially that, unless we have really learned to be poor in spirit, the material world can dominate and tyrannize over us, we can become the slaves of our flesh, and the loveliness of God's earth can turn for us into an evil beauty like a lovely face ravaged by greed and cruelty and lust.

Here then, especially, we need to be prepared; but it is a preparation which must necessarily be a long proc- ess. We shall not become poor in spirit suddenly, when danger most acutely threatens. It is when God's yoke seems light and His presence near that we need to school ourselves to meet the darkness; and to school ourselves, not by occasional dramatic renunciations but by constant daily attention to His will in tiny things.

Mary's Answer for Our Troubled Times

"Seek ye first the kingdom of Heaven":[16] if at every moment, we consult His will for us, if when life's gracious things come to us, we refer them back to Him in gratitude and love, and when difficulties arise, we turn to Him also in obedience and love, then we are learning how to see the material world as His world and not ours, and material things as His gifts and not our creatures. And so we can hope to be able to obey, even though it must be done instantly, even though it must be in darkness, when the time comes for us to flee into Egypt in our turn.

But when Herod was dead, we are told, there again appeared an angel to Joseph in Egypt, saying: "Arise, and take the Child and His mother and go into the land of Israel: for they are dead that sought the life of the Child."[17] There is a striking parallelism of circumstance. Again it is night, and Joseph asleep, and the words are almost identical, so that the similarity underlines the contrast: no longer a question of a flight, but of a glad return, and the reason given: they are dead that sought the life of the Child.

[16] Matt. 6:33.
[17] Matt. 2:20.

Mary shows us how to bear sudden losses

Those who have learned how to love the harshness as well as the tenderness of Love, to greet with gratitude the buffetings of God, come in the end to a state in which poverty of spirit is perfect in them, and greed and possessiveness are dead in them: they are dead that sought the life of the child in them, the newborn of God, and so they are free to return. They are free to return to the world to love the world, to gather all God's creatures into the embrace of their love, because God's creatures can no longer endanger their love of God; they can only help to express it.

So often the saints' lives follow this pattern: first the flight, the darkness, and the searching for God; but then the return to the world of men, the search for men, and the fulfillment of the love of God in the continuation of God's work for men. That is indeed the essence of Christian mysticism: it can never be content with a solitary absorption in God on the mountaintop, unaware of the poor misguided worldlings who people the plains below; for the Word was made flesh and dwelt among us,[18] and it is idle to say that you love God and are seeking God if you have no interest in the beings

[18] John 1:14.

Mary's Answer for Our Troubled Times

God loves so well that He made Himself one of them in order to die for them. There are indeed saints who are hermits and solitaries just as there are saints who work in the slums and hovels of the great cities; but all of them alike are fired by the same spirit, the same love; all of them alike share in Christ's redeeming care for the world.

And we who live in the plains, and who at best catch only the faintest echoes of the divine self-revealings which are given high above us — can we have any part in this rediscovery of the earth and this redeeming work? To all of us there must come sometimes — and to most of us there will come often — the same command to leave our belongings, to leave something that we treasure, and to go out into the darkness: not in any dramatic way, probably, will we hear this summons, but in the small events we tend to think of as our share of life's misfortunes, missing their divine message. If we see them for what they really are, in the light of this divine abandonment of home to bring back those who flee from God, then in us, too, they will gradually work a transformation; gradually they will lessen the hold of selfishness and greed upon our hearts; gradually they will make it more possible for us to love the things we like to think we love, and then perhaps to enlarge the boundaries of our love, to begin to love the things to which hitherto we had been indifferent or hostile; and so in the end, in our more pedestrian fashion, we shall be doing something of the same sort as the saints: we shall be learning to see the earth anew.

But this discovery of a new earth is not the final return, the final liberation. Still, so long as we are here, we remain the banished children of Eve: our home is elsewhere. And when we think of the flight into Egypt, we should think not only of a time when we can be fit to return to earth, but of a time when we can be fit to enter Heaven: we should pray not only for a love that is big enough to include the whole world, but for a love that is pure enough to meet God. For only then is the darkness really and fully over; only then is the exile ended, the day of the dark powers that sought our life really done: when God's mercy takes us to the land where darkness has no entrance, no dominion; the land where there is no loss, no sorrow, and no homesickness, but only the light and wonder of the eternal Presence, the glory and gaiety and peace of God.

The loss of the Child Jesus in the Temple

Mary shows us how to love others rightly

And not finding Him, they returned into Jerusalem, seeking Him.

Luke 2:45

There is a mysterious element in this story of the loss of the Child Jesus in Jerusalem which at first sight is very baffling. They go up to the city for the festival with their kinsfolk and acquaintances. The feast over, the caravan starts out on the return journey. Jesus, now a boy of twelve, is left considerable freedom, and it is not until the night that His parents realize that He is not with the pilgrimage. They hurry back to Jerusalem, dread in their hearts. They find Him in the temple, listening to the doctors of the law and asking them questions — a not unusual scene, except for the astonishing wisdom of His words. And then, when His mother gently reproaches Him, He offers no word of apology for the distress He has caused them and hardly a word that could be called an explanation, since they fail to understand what He says to them.[19] How could He seem so callous?

[19] Luke 2:42-50.

His words affirm His divine sonship: there are claims upon Him far more exalted and far more demanding than theirs.

But the whole scene, also, is a revelation of divinity: the story goes on to tell us how He went back with them and was subject to them,[20] and yet here there is a sense of detachment which seems harsh and callous because He is not only Mary's *Child* but Mary's *God*, and God has austere lessons to teach. Later on, He was to feel abandoned by His Father on the Cross:[21] it was an essential part of His work on earth, His sacrifice. And she who is to share so closely in that work and that sacrifice must experience something of the same thing: the lesson must be learned. Certainly it was not learned immediately. You imagine her telling the story so many years later, looking back down the years to those far-off dreamlike days of His childhood: they understood not the word that was spoken to them, she says; but she kept all these things in her heart, until in the end, they became clear.

And what was the lesson she finally learned?

[20] Luke 2:51.
[21] Matt. 27:46; Mark 15:34.

Mary shows us how to love others rightly

In the last chapter, we were thinking of our attitude toward things; here we are led to think of our attitude toward persons. The love of material things can be merely greed and possessiveness, the lust for pleasure or profit or power; but the love of human beings can be these things also, and then it is not real love at all, although we may deceive ourselves into thinking it to be. Because of our selfishness, to love in this real and deep sense is not an easy thing, not something given, but a hard thing, a thing that we have to learn, to create. First, to love God; then to love others as coming from Him, as given to us by Him, as His other children: this is what we must learn if we are really to love. Here more than anywhere, greed and possessiveness turn beauty into ugliness and light into darkness.

For a human being is more valuable than all the things that the world contains put together; and it is by that that we can measure our responsibility toward Him. We are like children stumbling in the dark; and if God in His tenderness gives us another of His children to accompany and comfort and help us, we must cherish the gift more than all riches, but we must know the heaviness of our responsibility: we must be always at pains to keep it in God's sight and God's care.

Mary's Answer for Our Troubled Times

We need human love to help us on our way; but three things will destroy it and leave us bereft and lonely, and they are things to which we are very prone.

Greed will destroy it: greed which means loving persons for the sake of things, loving human beings only for what they can give us. It is Satan who offers things to Christ in the temptation:[22] God offers not things but Himself. He asked the two disciples, "What seek you?" and they answered, "Where dwellest Thou?"[23] They wanted not a *what* but a *who*. It is the same when Christ says to St. Thomas Aquinas, "Thou hast written well of me, Thomas; what reward wouldst thou have of me?" and he answers, "*Nihil nisi Te, Domine* ('Nothing, Lord, save Thyself')."[24]

It is easy indeed to see that this is the right scale of values; it is not always easy to act on it. Greed lies deep down in us, and it can assume forms; it can hide behind appearances, which easily deceive us and others, too. "Of course I love you: I would do anything in the world

[22] Matt. 4:9; Luke 4:7.

[23] John 1:38.

[24] Bernard Gui, *The Life of Saint Thomas Aquinas*, trans. Kenelm Foster, O.P. (Baltimore: Helicon Press, 1959), 43.

for you," we say. Yes, but why? Sometimes giving can be a form simply of pleasure-seeking, of self-indulgence. "I am only trying to show you how I love you," we say, when really we are snatching at a purely selfish sensuality of our own. "Look at all the things I have given you and done for you," we say, not realizing that it was simply because it gave us pleasure, or even — poor fools that we are — because it ministered to a sense of power. "Command that these stones be made bread":[25] but you cannot turn greed into the bread of love if the motive that drives you is itself greed; you can do it only by learning to love and obey every word that proceedeth from the mouth of God.[26]

Greed is selfishness grasping at what one desires; possessiveness is selfishness clinging to what one has; and each of them equally can destroy love. Motherhood is for us the symbol of a perfect love because it is perfectly selfless; but its very perfection makes the travesties of it the more terrible. Think of the possessive mother, clinging to her children long after the time has come for them to be independent, retarding their development,

[25] Matt. 4:3.
[26] Cf. Matt. 4:4.

frustrating their careers, preventing them from marrying: she is not loving at all; she is destroying the personalities she pretends to love. But the same can be true of wives and husbands; the same can be true of friends. Wherever there is the desire to dominate, to mold and fashion according to one's own ideas, wherever demands are absolute and unconditional, there is not love but destruction.

Human love can never be unconditional: in all things, we are only stewards, and here more than anywhere we are only stewards. Our model here especially must be Mary, the true mother — her whole vocation consisting in living for Christ's vocation: mothering Him in His childhood, looking after Him in His youth, and then, when her work for the time being is done and He is ready for His public life, withdrawing quietly into the background until she is needed again to sustain Him in His Passion.

But a third thing, too, can kill love, and it is idolatry. If you exalt the objects of your love until your picture is a false one, if you idealize them, if you project upon them your own ideal picture of your own ideal self, then you are loving not a real person but a dream. The result is inevitable: sooner or later, the difference between ideal and real obtrudes itself upon you. Then you feel disappointed, cheated; you feel quite unjustly that you have somehow been wronged. And so, what looked to you like love but never was turns to dislike: the unreal romance is over before it ever touched reality, and real love is still as remote from your heart as ever. . . .

What we need is real love of real people, to heal our loneliness; and that means seeing them as they really are, and loving that; and that, in its turn, means not worshiping them as flawless ideals and deities, but helping them, and being helped by them, to worship God. More than that, as long as a fictitious idealized love dominates your heart, it tends to exclude everything else: it is jealous, possessive, absorbing, and greedy; and because the fiction is so largely a self-projection, it tends to make you more and more of an egoist. It is not until you are finding not the sham love but the real love that you can begin to learn the austere but grand and essential lesson: that it is not just one being that you must love but all beings: you must love all life.

Perhaps, in order to learn that lesson properly, we sometimes need the hard schooling of disappointment and loneliness; and so God gives it to us as He gave it to Mary and Joseph. Christ was to know utter loneliness in the garden and on the Cross;[27] Mary must learn it now as she seeks Him sorrowing, and she must learn it in order to fulfill the second and crowning part of her destiny: to be the mother of all men.

But the universality of charity is not something confined to her; it is something enjoined on every Christian: we need the same lesson in our turn. So disappointment comes to us with a purpose: separation, the loss of love, the death of one we love, or the death of love itself. And it is then that we have to try not to grumble or rebel, but to learn from what is being done in us.

For we shall never love all beings unless we love God more than all beings — not necessarily with a greater emotional intensity, but with a greater loyalty of will. God is said to be a jealous God,[28] not because He will not allow us to have other loves, but because He will not have rivals. And if, in fact, we love other things in defiance of Him, or away from Him, as distractions from Him, then our love tends to turn sour and, in the end, to destroy itself. So again, as with material things, we need poverty of spirit — not in order that, where creatures

[27] Matt. 26:40, 27:46.
[28] Exod. 20:5.

are concerned, we may love less, or less intensely, but that our love may be real. The love of God, once again, is a question essentially not of emotion but of devotion of the will: to love God more than anything else means essentially to love His will, effectively, more than any claim of any creature. Love with your whole heart; but make sure that your heart is given to God. Then you are giving the one you love something greater than a purely human love: you are giving a love which is indwelt by God; you are loving not only with your own love, but with God's.

He was twelve years old: we are given this lesson by Christ the Boy. It is a pity that nowadays, while Christianity has at Christmas its devotion to the infancy of Christ and always its devotion to the Christ-Man, the Redeemer, the devotion to the youthful Christ is so largely lost. Youth has lovely qualities. It has a freshness and charm, a shy grace, a clarity of vision, a sincerity, that later years can never recapture.

But it has something else. "The thoughts of youth are long, long thoughts":[29] there is a quality also of remoteness, as though the attention were half-directed

[29] Henry Wadsworth Longfellow, "My Lost Youth."

to some world unseen, the heart in some way withdrawn from the immediate phenomenal world even though then, coming back to it, the youthful heart seems to give the world something of its own urgent vitality. So it is Christ the Boy who teaches His mother to realize, "This Child is not mine, but God's." And He teaches us, in our turn, to say of all those we love, "These are not mine, but God's."

The first essential is that, like Christ in the temple, we should be near to the Father; the second, that with those we love, we should be near the Father together; for only so can we find freedom from greed and possessiveness and idolatry. When we are babies, we need other human beings all the time to look after us; and again when we are grown up, we need other human beings, and know our need; it is boyhood that is independent. And so we need the lesson of Christ the Boy, not to give us back a natural independence of temperament and heart which is not proper to adulthood, but to show us the supernatural counterpart of it, to touch creatures very gently lest we destroy them and ourselves.

Mary kept all these things in her heart, until the lesson became clear in the fullness of her wisdom. It is for us to ask her to give us a share in that wisdom; for her motherhood of men, her concern for all men, is certainly something in which we are called to share, and if we lack it, we shall only harm those we try to cherish.

There is one final lesson. They sought Him sorrowing, but in the end, they found Him; after three days, they found Him. It is like the three days in the tomb.[30] There are three days of darkness, but then the light; three days of death, but then the Resurrection. At first sight, you would say that this lesson taught by the Boy Christ is a purely harsh and austere one; but that is not its ending. In the end, it tells us that although for long days and months and years, you seem to be bereft of God, to have lost God, and you seem in vain to have sought Him sorrowing, still you must be of good heart: the search will not be in vain in the end. "They found Him . . . and He went down with them, and came to Nazareth." As with human love, so with divine love, there is first the lesson to be learned — the loneliness, the disappointments, and the sorrow that can teach us not to be greedy — but then there is the union, the companionship, that nothing can shatter, that even death cannot dissolve. For long years, perhaps, there is

[30] Matt. 12:40.

the desert, but then the joy of Nazareth, the House of Bread — and the breaking of bread together is the symbol of all the warmth and hospitality of home.

So here in the temple, He is saying in effect as He said explicitly later on: "Seek and ye shall find";[31] and when, after all the trials and discouragements, you are ready at last to love Him, you will find Him. And He will go down with you as He went down with Mary and Joseph, to Nazareth, and will give you in full measure, as He gave them — and everlastingly — His companionship, joy, and peace.

[31] Matt. 7:7; Luke 11:9.

Mary shows us how to answer suffering with love

*Go forth, ye daughters of Zion, and see
the king in the diadem wherewith his mother
crowned him in the day of his espousals.*

Song of Solomon 3:11

The way to Golgotha lies through the narrow, torrid, dusty streets of the city. You think of the jostling, jeering crowd, the noise, and the tumult; and then in the midst of it all, it is as if a silence falls as Jesus meets His mother: a private silence for these two alone as everything else is blotted out and they are conscious only of each other. (That concentration of gaze, that rapt and exclusive attention, is what our daily prayer ought to be.) They cannot speak, and so their sorrow is the greater.

And for Mary, it is a double sorrow: the mother's sorrow, watching the torments of the Son her body bore, and the girl's sorrow, flinching from the revelation of naked evil and cruelty destroying innocence and beauty and love. A double sorrow, but yet she is silent; it is not for her to find an emotional outlet for her grief, for she is here because of Him: she is here to fulfill her vocation as mother by helping Him to fulfill His as Savior: she is here to crown Him in the day of His espousals to the sorrows of man.

Mary's Answer for Our Troubled Times

There is a sharp contrast here between His mother and the women of Jerusalem to whom He spoke:[32] and the contrast is in the fact that He spoke. They love Him and sorrow for Him, but their sorrow seems too noisy, as though there is an element of self-pity in it, as though they are, in fact, calling attention to themselves, and instead of consoling Him, they look to Him to console them. In Mary is the silence of strength, and so she can give Him the strength of her silence: it is what she is there to do. In her, there are the two contradictory agonies: the longing to save Him from His unbearable agony and the effort to help Him to finish His work; and it is the second that she must do, giving Him to the world on the Cross as she has given Him to the world in the stable.

That is the first thing that Mary shows us. If her heart had been filled with a soft sentimental pity, she would not have helped, but would have hindered. Human love helps when it is within the framework of vocation, when it expresses the will of God. A mother's vocation is fulfilled when she offers her son to God, to life, and to his own destiny; it is ruined when she clings

[32] Luke 23:28.

to him for her own sake on the plea of saving him from hurt. "Go forth and see the king in the diadem wherewith his mother crowned him." And this is the crowning: her offering of her Son to the Father, her strengthening of her Son for the kingship of the Cross.

For the very offering is itself a help to Him, comforting and gladdening Him. For her, the meeting can be only agony: and John and Mary Magdalene must have tried to restrain her, while she insisted, "I must be with my Son; He will have need of me." And so she shows us a second thing: we are not merely to avoid confusing true pity with sentimental pity; we are to keep clear the distinction between true pity and self-pity. We, for our part, are not often asked to shoulder very heavy crosses perhaps, but the small ones come our way, and they fill us with self-pity; they make us yearn for and expect and perhaps demand sympathy until, in the end, we make others miserable in their turn. It is then that we should think of this scene, compare our noisy lamentations with this silence, our emotional wallowings with this strength, our wasted opportunity with this glory.

He had need of her; He has need, St. Paul tells us, of us, too. At Mass the priest raises the chalice in offering to God, and with it the lives, the work, the joys and pains of his people: and similarly, in every moment of trouble, there is the material not of self-pity but of self-offering as a part of Christ's offering: not only a completion now of His work,[33] but a lightening then of His load. It was not only Simon of Cyrene who eased the weight from His shoulders:[34] it was all those from His mother onward, all those then present and those to come, whose love consoled and strengthened Him. To turn a small trial into a trough of self-pity is to make it and ourselves still more petty; to share it thus with Him is to turn it, however small it may be, into a thing of grandeur, a giving of life.

And in Simon there is a further lesson for us. They *constrained* one Simon of Cyrene. . . . He was not eager to help; he hated the idea of helping; but he was forced. And what followed then? Christ had said, "My yoke is sweet and my burden light";[35] He had said when the woman touched His garment, "Virtue hath gone out from me."[36] It is unthinkable that virtue did not go out

---

[33] Cf. Col. 1:24.

[34] Matt. 27:32; Mark 15:21; Luke 23:26.

[35] Matt. 11:30.

[36] Luke 8:46.

also from the wood's touch, and that Simon, having begun in reluctance, did not end in joy, finding the wood sweet indeed and the burden light.

Good people are so often worried and distressed because, they say, they feel no devotion; they feel no love of God in their hearts, no readiness to suffer anything for Him, no zest for sacrifice. Then they have to be told that feelings are of no account: devotion is a question not of feelings but of will.

True, the emotions can be a great strengthening for the will: you work better when you are emotionally full of zest for the work; you work with more energy when you are happy and sanguine and your heart is in it. And there are times when God gives the emotional zest in His service to show us that His burden is light and to help us to form the habit of working for Him with vigor and constancy. But if He takes the joy away and gives us fatigue and boredom; if our hearts feel dead within us; if everything connected with His service seems purposeless and futile and perhaps cruel: then, provided we go on with the thing to be done, have we cause for despair or depression? On the contrary, it is then that we can show, and know, that we really are devoted. It is then that we can show, and know, that it is really God we love and not His gifts, and that love, for that very reason, can grow to its perfection; for love and devotion are not in the emotions but in the will.

Devotion, St. Thomas tells us, means the will to give oneself readily to God's service; and he goes on to show how devotion and love are reciprocal causes: charity causing devotion, since love makes one ready to serve one's friend, and devotion feeding charity, since friendly deeds safeguard and deepen friendship.[37] Whenever you in fact do what God tells you, then, you are growing in the love of God, no matter what your feelings may be.

"Fill the waterpots with water; and they filled them to the brim":[38] that is the only thing that matters; they did what they were told; they filled the waterpots, and they did it thoroughly — they filled them to the brim. And so the water was changed into wine; and so Simon's reluctance was turned into joy in the end; and so every act of obedience, however dry or dead the heart may feel, safeguards and deepens love in the soul.

But good people worry again because they say, "I never become any better; I go on week after week and

[37] *Summa Theologica*, II-II, Q. 82, art. 1, 2.
[38] John 2:7.

year after year committing the same sins, being equally unsuccessful at my attempts at prayer, never apparently becoming any less selfish, never apparently drawing any nearer to God. . . ." Are they so sure? What they ought to ask themselves is, "Do I equally go on week after week and year after year doing the same hard things for God, keeping for His sake the many other commandments that are often hard for me, going doggedly on trying to pray, going doggedly on trying to help other people?" And if the answer is yes (as it is), then they should know that whatever the surface appearances and disappointments may be, love is growing within them.

We live our lives at many different levels; and the events on the surface we can see and assess, but we may know little or nothing of what is going on deep down beneath the surface. If nature has made you choleric, you will no doubt go on losing your temper; if nature has made you lethargic, you will no doubt go on being lazy. But what do these things matter if, at the same time, charity is being fed in your soul by devotion, as friendship is safeguarded and deepened by friendly deeds?

They constrained one Simon of Cyrene. And perhaps God sometimes constrains those who love Him but think they do not love Him, so that in the doing of the work — the bearing of the cross He gives them — their love may grow and deepen although they remain unaware of it, until in the end, they find that beneath the apparent dryness and sterility, great things have been going forward in them and holiness has been born.

But it is not only God's cross that we are called to share, but those of His other children, too; and here also the same thing applies. The question is not whether we are emotionally eager to help (although if at any time we are, it is a great gift), but whether, in fact, we do help. And in the last resort, these crosses are all the one Cross: to help other men, out of charity, is to help God in His agony; and to help God is to help the race of men. So it is that even the smallest action of this sort can have a cosmic significance. Wherever in the midst of the noise, heat, and bustle of the world there falls a moment of silent sympathy, the giving of comfort and strength for the doing of God's will, there the redemption is operative and the wounds of the world are being healed.

"Till the day break and the shadows retire," we read in the Song of Solomon, "I will go to the mountain of myrrh and to the hill of frankincense":[39] myrrh for

[39] Song of Sol. 4:6.

Christ's burial, the myrrh the Magi brought.[40] And on that final journey into the darkness, His mother remained with Him, accompanying Him all the way, staying with Him until the end. And before the daybreak, there must be the heartbreak. But the daybreak came, the dawn of Resurrection, and then the sorrows that had gone before remained only as the material of the new and never-ending joy.

So it can be with all His followers in their turn: to take up the crosses He sends as readily, as devotedly as possible; to bear them with Him and for Him; and to go on unflaggingly until the day breaks and the shadows retire, to go on, if necessary, even to the mountain of myrrh, to the darkness and the burial. That is the way to know in the end something of the joy that flooded, so inexplicably, the soul of Simon. It is the way to know something of that far greater and more inexpressible joy of that other, later, meeting of Son and mother, when the day indeed had broken, the dawn indeed had come, and there was only joy for them now and the shared happiness of their love, the love that, having gone down in silence together to the very depths of human agony,

[40] John 19:39; Matt. 2:11.

now rose together to the heights of more than human glory — to that joy of which no tongue can tell, but which is promised in degree in God's mercy to all those who, in company with Mary, try to love, follow, and serve her Son.

Mary shows us how to bear even the heaviest crosses

When Jesus therefore had seen His mother and the disciple whom He loved, He saith to His mother, "Woman, behold thy son."

John 19:26

When a hurt or a sorrow, a loss or a cross, is stated in words, the words seem to make the facts more real and more cruel, more hard to bear: there is a flat finality about them — "I am going away"; "I don't love you"; "She is dead" — that is like the tolling of a knell in the mind and heart. Mary had been standing afar off, but now she drew near. And would He now at the end have a word to speak to His mother?

Yes, and it was concerned with her comfort, His friend's care of her; yet at the same time, it drove the sword deeper because it drew her life with Him to a close: He was leaving her.

And yet this word of dereliction for her has at the same time been taken throughout the ages as the symbol for the grand — universal — enlargement of her vocation as mother: her motherhood of men. Woman, behold thy son John — but with him also the whole race of men: they are thy sons because they are my brothers. And her work now will be to care for and cherish them as she had cared for and cherished Him; to help them fulfill their vocations as she had helped Him fulfill His.

Yet it might well seem that this was not the moment for new glories and new responsibilities, this hour of her final dereliction. Why should it not rather have been at Pentecost, when the Church was established by the indwelling of the Spirit, and her own special work within the Church's life might therefore be thought to have formally begun? Perhaps the answer is simply that she, for her part, had no need to wait, as the Apostles needed to wait: she had already now — and this moment was the final consummating lesson — all the knowledge and experience she needed.

But there is something more. Here, at this moment, she is stripped of all human resources and thrown back entirely upon God. Later, John will be there to help her; others will be there to help her. No one can help her at this moment when she has eyes only for her dying Son. "All ye who pass by the way, attend and see if there be any sorrow like to my sorrow":[41] there is no prop, no help, and no comfort that can have any meaning. And in the fact that it is indeed at that moment of utter

[41] Lam. 1:12.

negation that this universal motherhood is given to her, there is a great lesson for us.

When prayer seems most hopeless, it may well be most fruitful; when the search for God and the attempt to love God seem most futile and barren, they may well be most creative. Why? Because if then we turn to God in humility, knowing our failure, we make it possible for Him to work in us, and under His creative touch, the soul comes to life, the flame is kindled, even though we remain unconscious of it. At other times, our efforts may, in fact, be egoistic and self-reliant, or greedy of reward, and then we fail, however convinced we may be of our success.

"A man," writes Thomas Merton, "who is not stripped and poor and naked within his own soul will always unconsciously do the works he has to do for his own sake rather than for the glory of God. He will be virtuous not because he loves God's will but because he wants to admire his own virtues. But every moment of the day will bring him some frustration that will make him bitter and impatient, and in his impatience he will be discovered. . . .

"To say that I am made in the image of God is to say that love is the reason for my existence: for God is love.

Mary's Answer for Our Troubled Times

Love is my true identity. Selflessness is my true self. Love is my true character. Love is my name. . . .

"I who am without love cannot become love unless Love identifies me with Himself. But if He sends His own Love, Himself, to act and love in me and in all that I do, then I shall be transformed, I shall discover who I am and shall possess my true identity by losing myself in Him. And that is what is called sanctity."[42]

When, at the end, we see our lives for what they really are, against the pure light of eternity, shall we see them as largely a sham Christianity, perhaps more or less respectable, law-abiding, kindly, but really, underneath, always clinging to the self-will which is the root of evil, our very piety colored by our pride? Or shall we be able to say that in spite of all our sin, we did try to make God the master in everything, did try to love His will in everything even though we constantly failed, did try to take the "leap in the dark" and tumble our lives into His hands as a total gift? That, at any rate, is the one essential thing we must do. He that loseth his life shall find it.[43] With us, as with Christ, there is first the death

[42] *Seeds of Contemplation,* 44, 46.

[43] Matt. 10:39; Luke 9:24.

and only then the resurrection; with us, as with Mary, there is first the nakedness and dereliction of spirit, and only then the flowering of the divine vocation.

How is it to be done?

We have to go down into His death. We have to go down into the darkness within us and recognize the evil within us, the pride and the egoism; we have to recognize how they color and taint all the things that we do, and how powerless we are to turn the darkness into light. (There is only one thing, says St. Thomas, of which man is the first cause: evil.) And then, in the nakedness of that self-knowledge, we can give ourselves wholly into the hands of the Spirit, and the Spirit can re-create us, for in the death of pride and egoism, the soul is reborn as a child.

Jacques Maritain[44] has some wise words on the parables of the man counting his resources before building a tower and the king counting his army before meeting his enemy in the field:[45] "Which means to say," he writes, "before setting to work for God and to fight against the Devil, first calculate your forces; and if you

[44] French Thomist philosopher (1882-1973).
[45] Luke 14:28-32.

consider yourself well enough equipped to begin, you are a fool, because the tower to be built costs an outrageous price, and the enemy coming out to meet you is an angel, before whom you are of no account. Get to know yourself so well that you cannot contemplate yourself without flinching. Then there will be room for hope. In the sure knowledge that you are obliged to do the impossible, and that you can do the impossible in Him who strengthens you, then you are ready for a task which can be performed only through the Cross."

So, at times, God takes away all props, all help, from His children; leaves them apparently bereft; and reduces them apparently to failure and desolation, so that sometimes they seem to have no faith left in Him, in themselves, or in anything at all. But it is all done with a purpose: for when, at last, there is nothing left but dry bones, if they turn to Him in humility, He can make the dry bones live, and bring success out of failure, and hope and achievement out of despair. "Prophesy concerning these bones, and say to them: 'Ye dry bones, hear the word of the Lord . . . "Behold I will send spirit into you and you shall live. And I will lay sinews upon you, and will cause flesh to grow over you, and will cover you with skin: and I will give you spirit and you shall live, and you shall know that I am the Lord." ' "[46] When failure comes upon us, when we are tempted to depression or despair, it is of these dry bones that we should think, and see whether, in fact, there is some work waiting to be done for God. We should turn to Him and beg Him to work in us in spite of our frailties and failures. And so in us, as they do in their greater ways in the saints, failures and frustrations become creative.

But there is here a perennial difficulty which confronts many of us if we try to put all this into effect: we have to confess to ourselves a lack of will; we cannot even bring ourselves to will to begin on what needs to be done. In other words, we cannot conquer our sloth. We must, of course, be sure that we are not confusing sloth with physical or mental fatigue, with nerve-strain, or with laziness or indolence. *Devotion* means the will to give oneself readily to God's service; *sloth* means a refusal or, perhaps more accurately, a culpable inability to achieve the will to give oneself readily to His service. A culpable inability: this is the noonday demon of the psalm.[47] This is the boredom, the lack of volition, that

[46] Ezek. 37:4-6.

[47] Ps. 90:6 (Revised Standard Version: Ps. 91:6).

assails one in the afternoon of the day or the afternoon of life, the middle-day, the middle-years; the boredom that marks that second stage in God's service, when the freshness and lyricism have gone, the emotional enthusiasm is a thing of the past, and what was once easy and exciting and rewarding is now nothing but a hard grind, a clinging to God and His work only with "naked intent of the will." How, then, can we turn to Him in our failures if we lack the will to turn? How can we take Him our failures and frustrations if we lack the will to go to Him at all?

Perhaps in this scene at the foot of the Cross, a double answer is given to us. There must surely be, first of all, in Mary that same unbreakable concentration of attention that we saw on the road to Calvary. There was also, in the second place, the giving of this new duty, this new work: the mothering of humanity.

The concentration of gaze: we would not be slothful if we lived habitually and familiarly in His presence. If we refused to live on the surface of life, to float placidly in the conventionalized religious shallows; if we freed ourselves, at whatever cost, from the frenzied tempo of modern life and taught ourselves to be still, to pray; then, in that prayer-stillness, we would begin to be aware of the distant horizons which give this world its meaning. And so we would begin to do the work of every day in God and with God and for God; and His companionship would vitalize our wills and liberate us from our sloth.

But then there is also the work for humanity. It is more difficult, as St. John pointed out, for a man to love God, whom he sees not, than to love his brother whom he sees.[48] But to be spurred to one kind of initiative and activity is to find it easier to embark on others. (It is, of course, possible, consciously or unconsciously, to make activity in the world — even the most beneficent — a screen, an escape from the presence of God, but it need not be so.) In these days, it is hardly possible for anyone to remain unaware of the desperate needs of the world; but to the Christian, these needs must appear in an especially forcible and dramatic form. For Christianity points us through death to life, through darkness to light. But it would seem as though the world today were facing in exactly the opposite direction; as though, deep down within, there were the will-to-death; as though the world were dying because it wants to die.

[48] 1 John 4:20.

Mary's Answer for Our Troubled Times

Sometimes you find this death-wish explicit and complete, expressed in individual — or race — suicide. More often you find it in a paralysis of the will, a despair which destroys initiative. There is an expression of this in the breakdown of the structure and machinery of society, a breakdown which goes very deep, so that the attempt to stem it by frenzied legislation and short-term policies is but tinkering. There is an expression of it, too, in the passive acceptance of encroaching totalitarianism. And there is an expression of it in the hatred of beauty and wisdom and all the things that bring life to the spirit.

All these things are simply a cry to the dark gods of destruction, "Crucify us, crucify us!"[49] And why is there this adoration of death? We know in our own lives that insofar as we give ourselves to pride and falsehood, to cruelty and greed, we call down death and disintegration upon ourselves; but there is in us that which lusts after that disintegration, and it will conquer us unless we learn that life is to be found not in self-worship but in Love-worship, that our name is love. So it is with a society which refuses that lesson: it may go on perhaps

[49] Cf. Luke 23:21.

for centuries living on the surface, forgetting the deep places, content without God; but sooner or later the shell cracks, the hollowness is revealed, and there is nothing left but the mocking grin of despair.

But what if we ourselves, despite our Christianity, are in the same position? We must go back to this same scene on Calvary, and see again God's self-revelation there. "Jerusalem, Jerusalem," He had said once before, "thou that stonest the prophets and killest them that are sent to thee, how often would I have gathered thy children as the hen doth gather her chickens under her wing, and thou wouldst not."[50] God's love is far greater than any human categories; and His fatherhood does not exclude those qualities we associate more especially with motherhood: the gentleness, the tenderness, the intuitive understanding and the sympathy. There are men who have to be both father and mother to their motherless children; and sometimes they do, in fact, develop these other qualities and, in so doing, give us a clue to what the love of God in its fullness means. And here again, at the foot of the Cross, the same fact is taught us in the bestowal upon us of His own mother: it

[50] Luke 13:34.

is God saying, in effect, "You can come to me like that, as to a mother."

And so the first lesson is deepened and reinforced: we cannot let ourselves be desperate and despondent, because we must be conscious of God's enfolding arms, God's motherly care and understanding and sympathy. We know that God's wisdom will send trials and derelictions. But in the light of this lesson, we know that they are sent only to be creative for us and in us. And we know that just as out of Mary's dereliction came this greatness and this glory, so, too, out of our small tribulations can come a sharing, in our small way, in her work: an ability to have something of her wise and tender and perceptive care for the people or the things God gives us to cherish.

It is for us, then, only to try to take these trials and derelictions when they come without bitterness, without gloom, as a way in which our egoism can be exercised and our hearts liberated to live in God and share God's power. And then, too, we shall know in the end of the joy of the final outcome. "A woman, when she is in labor, hath sorrow because her hour is come; but when she hath brought forth the child, she remembereth not the anguish, for joy that a man is born into the world."[51] Mary had brought Him forth into life, and now on Golgotha, she watched over His death, His journey into the other greater life, and soon her sorrow, too, would be turned into greater joy. So for us, too, if only we have faith and courage enough: "You now have sorrow, but I will see you again and your heart shall rejoice; and your joy no man shall take from you."[52]

[51] John 16:21.
[52] John 16:22.

The removal of Jesus' body from the Cross

Mary shows us how to
draw good from suffering

*And Rizpah the daughter of Aiah took haircloth and spread
it under her upon the rock from the beginning of the harvest
till water dropped upon them out of heaven; and suffered
neither the birds to tear them by day nor the beasts by night.*

2 Kings 21:10
(Revised Standard Version:
2 Samuel 21:10)

The Pietà, the representation of God's mother holding her dead Son in her arms, is a symbol of the self-imposed powerlessness of God in the hands of men. Christ's body was still divine in death as it is divine in life — divine, yet robbed of all its human, natural powers: taken down from the Cross by the soldiers, held in Mary's arms, wrapped by Joseph of Arimathea in the linen cloth, and carried to burial.[53]

In the Mass, too, God makes Himself a passive thing, to be held and moved and broken by the fingers of the priest. And you see that powerlessness most appallingly manifest in the Black Mass of the Satanists. But to every human being God gives a similar terrifying power over Himself: the power to reject Him if he will. Power is a commonplace — and, to some, an attractive — thing; yet how terrifying also, when we reflect upon it. A man has power over himself, over other men, over other

[53] Matt. 27:59.

creatures, and over God Himself: he has power, in small ways or in great, to change history; he has power to save or ruin souls.

The Pietà is the symbol of God's love. If none of His creatures had free will, what a neat and tidy place the world would be: all things joining together in an unsullied song of praise to God; no problem of evil, no problem of pain, no problem of Hell, and no hatred. No hatred, but also no love, no friendship: and it was love and friendship that God wanted most of His creation; it was to make love possible that He gave some of His creatures freedom.

The terrible choice is given. You can put power at the service of love; then it is creative, beneficent, and lovely, as it is in God. Or you can divorce power from love; then it becomes destructive, evil, and ugly. Jacob Boehme[54] held that such a divorce of power from love is, in fact, the root evil; and we may well agree with him, we who have seen power in complete corruption, with all its tyranny, ruthlessness, cruelty, and dark malignance.

This does indeed follow inescapably from the first primordial sin of pride: the refusal to obey is itself a

[54] German Lutheran theosophical author (1575-1624).

determination to exercise power autonomously, independently of God — but if independently of God, then independently of love. And so man's paternal dominion over the world, his family, was lost to him. The darkest pages in the world's history, and in the Church's history, are those which tell of the horrible effects of man's lust for power and abuse of power.

It is easy to use power over others irresponsibly: for the pleasure or prestige or self-aggrandizement to be found in its exercise. It is easy to use it selfishly: turning people into means instead of ends, means to our own profit, our own good, instead of setting out ourselves to achieve theirs. There may be a temptation to use it cruelly, for the dark pleasure that cruelty itself gives; or with that particular sort of inhumanity which puts more store on patterns than on persons, on the neatness and efficiency of a scheme instead of on the uniqueness of every individual soul. Power, in this sense of authority, corrupts whenever it turns to possessiveness, jealousy, petty tyrannies, officiousness, or impersonality; and it corrupts for the same reason: it is divorced from love.

It is the same with other forms of power. There is mental power: the cleverness that can be used for vanity for the discomfiture of others, for the perversion of truth, or for the destruction of souls; the critical faculty that can be used proudly, rashly, and destructively; and the wit that can turn to cruelty. There is the power given by those personal qualities — charm, beauty, attractiveness — which engender love, and therefore vulnerability, in others and which, again, can be used so irresponsibly, so heartlessly, and so cruelly.

All power implies a corresponding responsibility; and the greater the power, the greater the responsibility, because the greater the danger.

And so we come back to the Pietà; for the greatest and most terrible of all powers is this power that God Himself gives us, to love Him or hurt Him. One of the fearful things about power is that we cannot measure the effect of the abuse of it: if we wantonly hurt other human beings, we know that evil will come of it, but we cannot foretell the extent of the evil. If we wantonly hurt God, we can only suppose that the resultant evil must be immeasurably magnified: it is the whole purpose of creation that we are then attempting to frustrate, since we are refusing to God the primary purpose of His creation of man. And because He has told us clearly that to sin against His creatures is to sin against

Him,[55] we must see all abuse of power in this light, as taking on something of the character of this evil; and so we cannot be indifferent to the smallest manifestation of it.

Yet the power is given to us; we cannot be rid of it. Authority has to be exercised; personal gifts have to be used. How can we attempt to make sure that our use of power will not, in fact, be an abuse? Only by making ourselves powerless before God, as the dead body of Christ was powerless; only by becoming "stripped and poor and naked" within our own souls, so that the Spirit can invest us with His divine power and transform our impulses and cure our pride.

We live in an age of power. The vast resources which science puts at man's disposal are paralleled by the mighty concentrations of economic and political power which characterize our world. But on the other hand, there are thinkers who look now to the coming of a new age in the world out of our present chaos, an age of the Spirit, an age of inwardness in which men, turning again to contemplation, turning away from the frenzied pursuit of superficial ends and opening their hearts to

[55] Cf. Matt. 25:40, 45; Acts 9:4.

the indwelling of the Spirit, the indwelling of love, will bring about a deep revolution in our ways of thought and the ways of life.

For just as at the first Pentecost, the coming of the Spirit into the hearts of the Apostles was the crowning and consummation of the work and sacrifice of the God-Man — the inward possession completing the outward teaching and example and Redemption which was the mission of the Son[56] — so now the renewed, redoubled activity of the Spirit in the Church and in the world would complete that redemptive work in the world by internalizing all that the Christian centuries have achieved in fashioning, defining, and elucidating the Christian way of life. There would be a great upsurge of charity throughout the world, so that power would go forth from men as it went forth from Christ, not through the words they speak but through the love in their hearts; God's law would no longer be something heard and if possible obeyed as an external ruling, but something deep within them, the rhythm of their hearts.

Certainly it is when you find men like that that you find power purely beneficent; and if the age of power is

[56] Acts 2:4; John 14:26.

not to go down into utter destruction, it must learn the way to this other and greater power: the power which flung the Apostles out of their hiding and into the streets to preach the wonderful works of God, the power that invested the Roman girl-saints and their followers in other ages and led them to defy the might and cruelty of secular tyranny, the power that has possessed all those who have sacrificed themselves for the good of humanity. Secular power may possibly unify a world through force; only love can unite a world in freedom.

"You call me Master, and Lord; and you say well, for so I am. If then I, being your Lord and Master, have washed your feet; you also ought to wash one another's feet. For I have given you an example, that as I have done to you, so you do also."[57] The pattern is there, the way power is to be used: not in arrogance and ruthlessness, but in fear and humility. "All power is given to me in Heaven and on earth":[58] but it led Him to lie naked and dead in the lap of His mother; for His work was to do the will of Him who sent Him,[59] and all His life was

[57] Cf. John 13:13-15.
[58] Matt. 28:18.
[59] Cf. John 4:34, 9:4.

a self-offering to His Father from whom alone the power came.

We shall not use our powers aright unless we use them in the spirit of Christ washing His disciples' feet; we shall not use our powers aright unless, like Him, we put them back into God's hands to be at His disposal. But if, at all times, we try to turn to God — to God our Father, in childlike trust and obedience; to God the Son, our friend, waiting to learn how we can fulfill friendship by sharing in His work and His sacrifice; and to God the Spirit within us, listening for that inner voice which instructs the heart, and begging Him to identify our wills with us — then we can know that our power is in better hands than ours, in hands that will never abuse it as ours would, because they are as gentle as they are strong.

There is something more. Rizpah sat guarding the bodies of her sons, "and suffered neither the birds to tear them by day nor the beasts by night." Mary held her Child in her arms in death as she had done in babyhood, the two moments of powerlessness. There is one use of power which is particularly divine and therefore particularly lovely: the use of power to protect or succor the powerless. To use the strength of your body to help those who are weak; to use the powers of your mind to help those who are less gifted; to use whatever material power or authority you may have to protect others; above all, to use the powers of your heart to bring comfort, strength, and hope to those in sorrow, pain, and distress: all this is power expressing love in deed.[60]

Always in the world there are men and women and children being torn by the evil birds of slander and scandal-mongering and pharisaism, by the wild beasts of cruelty, tyranny, and hatred. Always the poor and weak and defenseless are at the mercy of man's injustice and rapacity; the gentle are at the mercy of the ruthless, the humble at the mercy of the proud. When you support and defend them, you share with Mary in the sublimity of her vocation — and you share with her in her devotion to her Son, for inasmuch as these things are done to the least of His little ones, they are done to Him.[61]

But you must first take haircloth, like Rizpah, the haircloth of penitence and humility; you must first be stripped and poor and naked; or you will do these things for your own sake rather than for the glory of God. The

[60] Cf. 1 John 3:18.
[61] Cf. Matt. 25:40.

proud philanthropist can be one of humanity's worst enemies. He will use his gold for what seem to him to be good purposes, but, being proud, he will have no understanding of men's hearts and of men's needs, no real sympathy for their sufferings. His charity will have something in it of the inhumanity of a bureaucratic regimentation of benefits.

If ever your help has about it an atmosphere of condescension or impatience, it will not be following the divine pattern: you can only help as God helps if, like Him, you go down on your knees, knowing that this is not so much something you give as something you are given. Only to him who has nothing will much be given, that he may give to others. Only the poor in spirit can truly feed the hungry; only the naked can clothe the naked; only those who, having nothing, possess all things,[62] are given the power and the resources to harbor the harborless, to lead home the homeless and the outcast and the lost.

---

[62] 2 Cor. 6:10.

Mary shows us how to let God triumph over evils

*And he rolled a great stone to the door
of the sepulcher, and went his way.*

Matthew 27:60

A nd went his way: they are the words which close the Stations of the Cross, and there is a terrible sort of finality about them, like the clanging of a door upon an empty world. You think of the church on Good Friday, when the Presence has gone from it and it is now only a house, not a home. Yet that very emptiness, since, in fact, it is very far from final, only serves to underline for us the things we have been considering.

We have been thinking of freedom: freedom from fear, from the tyranny of material things, from possessiveness, from self-pity, from depression, from the abuse of power, and from all the various forms of egoism. And we have been thinking of the one essential key to all these forms of freedom: the sharing in Christ's death — stripped and poor and naked — that leads to the sharing in His life and His love.

"Know you not that we, who are baptized in Christ Jesus, are baptized in His death? For we are buried together with Him by Baptism into death; that as Christ is risen from the dead by the glory of the Father, so we also may walk in newness of life."[63] In Baptism, we are buried in Christ. We begin to live in newness of life, because it reverses the order of sin, of egoism: it restores that order whereby God, not our own ego, is at the center of our lives. And so we are re-established in the *ordo universi*, the total pattern of creation. For the self-centered man is isolated, separate, cut off from his roots in this and in other worlds; but the God-centered man is planted again in the universe, living again in rhythm with the sun and the stars and the earth, living again in harmony with the song of the spheres, because he is planted in the God of the universe.

But Baptism is not an end, but a beginning: it gives us the *power* to achieve, not the achievement. And we may fail. "He rolled a great stone to the door of the sepulcher and went his way." It is so easy to lose vision and love. God gives you an insight into reality, a glimpse of Himself that would take you deep into His love and far in His service; but superficialities and the world unlit by vision call to you, and you may roll a great stone between you and what you saw, and go your way, and the vision is lost.

[63] Rom. 6:3-4.

Mary shows us how to let God triumph

But *he* rolled the stone: it must always be we ourselves — it is never God — who will erect the barrier: the only obstacles are those we make ourselves. God is always pursuing us with His love; it is we who try to escape, to blot out the vision. We blot it out by prolonged, deliberate disobedience; we blot it out by open rebellion, by hatred, to which prolonged disobedience can lead; we blot it out by becoming hardened in indifference, which means indeed a gradual closing of all avenues to the greater world of eternity, a severing of all our roots, a stifling of all the deepest elements in our being, so that, in the end, unless we turn back again, desolation inescapably follows, the immovable separateness and loneliness of Hell.

And he rolled a *great* stone: God is not lightly lost to us; God is never lost to us so long as we go on trying, however unsuccessfully, to serve Him. The little imperfections, the transitory semideliberate failings, and the frailties: these can never be a great stone of separation. No sinfulness, however great, which leaves humility and love in the soul can ever be a great stone of separation. But good people imagine that God is lost to them because He *feels* remote from them; they blame themselves for loss of vision because it is dark night in their souls, but the dark night comes to them from God. The sinner is not an outcast from Christendom: he is at the very heart of Christendom, so long as there remains in him the will to turn to God, to go on searching for God and trying to serve Him.

And just as the loss of stability and comfort, of friends and family, even to utter dereliction, may be sent to us so that we may learn to love God and find life, so, too, the loss of a sense of His presence, the loss of His inner reassurances, and the loss of the joys of His service may be sent to us to ensure that we love Him and not His gifts, to ensure that we are indeed stripped and poor and naked and are not pretending to ourselves that we love Him when in reality we love only ourselves.

"In the beginning . . . the earth was void and empty, and darkness was upon the face of the deep; and the Spirit of God moved over the waters."[64] The tomb, the womb, the waters of chaos: these are the symbols for that nothingness, that self-annihilation of humility, out of which alone goodness and beauty can be created. We are to be buried with Christ so that we may live and move in a new kind of existence: we are to be stripped

[64] Gen. 1:1-2.

of all life, all resources, and all forms that are full of self, so that the Spirit may move over the waters of our chaos and re-create us, life springing anew from the womb, life springing anew from the tomb, the life of the new self which is the true self, identified with the self of Christ.

Then, as we saw before, we can hope to imitate Mary, not only in her motherhood, but in her enduring girl-hood, her enduring strangeness to evil, even though our story hitherto has been a story of squalor. For Christian-ity is precisely the religion which redeems humanity's squalors. When we lay ourselves bare to God's touch, it can never be to a mere negation, a formlessness, that we strip ourselves: we are never pure negation, like the primeval chaos; we are privation, the waters dark and turbulent with ugliness and evil. But God was made sin for our sakes:[65] it is into the depths of this squalor that the Word came; it is into the depths of this squalor that the Spirit comes to each individual soul, provided only that the sin can be transformed by creative sorrow.

He rolled a great stone to the door of the sepulcher; and yet, great though it was, "very early in the morning,

[65] 2 Cor. 5:21.

on the first day of the week . . . they found the stone rolled back."[66] The night seems so long and so relentless, the darkness so black and impenetrable, but swiftly in the end the light comes. You would say the evil was irredeemable, the pride too entrenched, the sloth more dazzling until it merges into the splendor of the light inaccessible; the song swelling and deepening until it merges into the harmony of the Uncreated Love.

And at the center of that splendor and radiance and happiness, there sits the Queen of the Seven Swords. And her song is still the song with which her life of motherhood began, and it is the song, too, of all those children whom her motherhood has helped to save:

> My soul doth magnify the Lord;
> And my spirit hath rejoiced in God my Savior;
> Because He hath regarded the humility of His
>   handmaid; for behold from henceforth all
>   generations shall call me blessed;
> For He that is mighty hath done great things to me;
>   and holy is His name.[67]

[66] Mark 16:2, 4.
[67] Luke 1:46-49.

Biographical note

Gerald Vann, O.P.

(1906-1963)

Born in England in 1906, Gerald Vann entered the Dominican Order in 1923 and, after completing his theological studies in Rome, was ordained a priest in 1929. On returning to England, he studied modern philosophy at Oxford and was then sent to Blackfriars School in Northhamptonshire to teach and later to serve as headmaster of the school and as superior of the community there. Tireless in his efforts to promote peace, he organized the international Union of Prayer for Peace during his tenure at Blackfriars.

Fr. Vann devoted his later years to writing, lecturing, and giving retreats in England and in the United States, including lecturing at Catholic University of America in Washington, DC. He wrote numerous articles and books, among them a biography of St. Thomas Aquinas, who influenced him greatly.

Fr. Vann's writings combine the philosophy and the theology of St. Thomas with the humanism emphasized in the 1920s and 1930s. His works reflect his keen understanding of man's relationship to God, his deep sensitivity to human values, and his compassionate understanding of man's problems and needs. Particularly relevant in today's divided world is his appeal for unity, charity, and brotherhood. His words reveal what it means today to fulfill the two greatest commandments: to love God and to love one's neighbor.

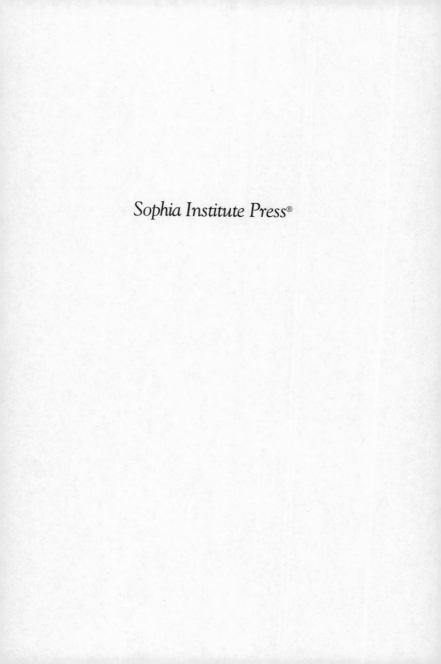

Sophia Institute Press®

Sophia Institute is a nonprofit institution that seeks to restore man's knowledge of eternal truth, including man's knowledge of his own nature, his relation to other persons, and his relation to God.

Sophia Institute Press® serves this end in numerous ways. It publishes translations of foreign works to make them accessible for the first time to English-speaking readers. It brings back into print books that have been long out of print. And it publishes important new books that fulfill the ideals of Sophia Institute. These books afford readers a rich source of the enduring wisdom of mankind.

Sophia Institute Press® makes these high-quality books available to the general public by using advanced technology and by soliciting donations to subsidize its general publishing costs.

Your generosity can help Sophia Institute Press® to provide the public with handsome editions of works containing the enduring wisdom of the ages. Please send your tax-deductible contribution to the address below.

The members of the Editorial Board of Sophia Institute Press® welcome questions, comments, and suggestions from all our readers.

For your free catalog, call:
Toll-free: 1-800-888-9344

or write:
Sophia Institute Press®
Box 5284
Manchester, NH 03108

Internet users may visit our website at
www.sophiainstitute.com

Sophia Institute is a tax-exempt institution as defined
by the Internal Revenue Code, Section 501(c)(3).
Tax I.D. 22-2548708.